Inscriptio in Circuitu Calicis.

Sacrum hunc Ca...
Antiquae pietatis Monument... ...infignem
aere perennari voluit q... ...aſervatur
Ric. Rawlinson. LL.D. æon. R.S.S.

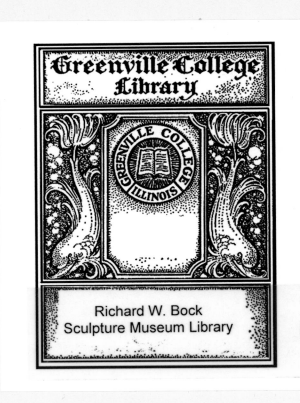

AFRO-PORTUGUESE IVORIES

TEXT BY W. P. FAGG, M. A.
DEPUTY KEEPER OF THE DEPARTMENT OF
ETHNOGRAPHY IN THE BRITISH MUSEUM
PHOTOGRAPHS BY W. & B. FORMAN

THIS BOOK IS DEDICATED TO THE UNKNOWN ARTISTS OF THE WEST COAST OF AFRICA, WHOSE WORK IS A MUTE WITNESS OF A VANISHED WORLD

FRO-PORTUGUESE IVORIES

BATCHWORTH PRESS • LONDON

DESIGNED AND PRODUCED BY ARTIA
for
BATCHWORTH PRESS

SPRING HOUSE • SPRING PLACE • LONDON NW 5
Printed in Czechoslovakia

BP 105 — S 554

CONTENTS

	Page
Introduction	VII
A Description of the Ivories	IX
The Ivories and their Place in African Art	XV
Bibliographical Note	XXIII
The Plates	XXV

Our warmest thanks are due to
Mr Adrian Digby,
without whose understanding and help this book
could not have been produced.

B. and W. Forman

YBRIDISM IN ART, IN THE SENSE OF fusion of the aesthetics of widely differing civilisations or cultures, is seldom very successful—Gandhara sculpture providing perhaps the most notable exception—and for this reason has been comparatively little studied. In Negro Africa, the impact of the European aesthetic (nearly always, it must be admitted, in a very debased form) has been almost uniformly devastating, particularly during the past century. This makes it all the more surprising that the hybrid style first comprehensively presented in this book should so long have escaped concentrated study, being regarded, following von Luschan's cavalier pronouncement of six decades ago, as simply a specialized variation of the style of Benin in what is now Western Nigeria.

The British Museum collection, which is here illustrated, is probably the largest and most representative in the world, few of the other museums of Europe possessing more than three or four pieces; but even in the British Museum the collection has only recently been segregated from the unrelated ivory work of Benin and eastern Yorubaland and separately exhibited.

The present essay is not designed to be definitive but to give some account of existing knowledge about what remains a somewhat myste-rious problem in African art history. In defining this problem, it will be well to begin by considering the nature of the traditional indigenous art of the African tribes, and secondly the nature of the changes normally wrought in that art by the different values introduced with European civilization.

THE SERIES OF IVORY OBJECTS—NUM-bering, probably, at least a hundred pieces—to which, for reasons which I shall state, I have given the name of 'Afro-Portuguese ivories' falls readily for the purposes of description into four groups, all of which are well represented in the British Museum collection. These are: (1) the pedestal cups; (2) the hunting horns; (3) the spoons and forks; and (4) miscellaneous objects such as the monstrous head in the British Museum and a powderflask in the Musée de Cluny. We may now consider these groups in detail.

THE CUPS

These normally consist of a more or less globular vessel (the upper half forming the lid) supported on a flaring foot, these basic forms being embellished with a great variety of ornament. Occasionally the whole may be carved in three pieces instead of two, a second and smaller globular compartment surmounting the first; or the flaring base, which often has several human and animal figures disposed more or less upright around it, may be absent, leaving the figures to support the bowl above.

Some have been carved from exceptionally large elephant tusks; the 'drum' of ivory which is the carver's raw material is necessarily selected from a point above, or only just including, the tip of the nerve cavity, that is about half-way along the tusk, and even the magnificent specimen illustrated in Plates 1–6 is therefore not taken from the thickest part.

So far, I have referred to these vessels by the broad and non-committal term 'cups'; their use and function are in fact an interesting subject for discussion. They have sometimes been described as chalices, with the suggestion that they were designed, to the order of Portuguese missionaries, for liturgical use as communion vessels. In a number of cases this might not seem altogether implausible, although the absence of religious subjects in the ornamentation (except in the case of the fine specimen belonging to the Newcastle-upon-Tyne Society of Antiquaries, at present on loan in the British Museum, the lowermost band of relief designs on which seems to include Biblical scenes such as Daniel in the den of lions) would in that case occasion some surprise. But a design such as that of the man whose genitals are attacked by a crocodile (Plate 3) seems positively unsuitable for this purpose, and there is one example, recently acquired by the Nigerian Museum, which, by reason of a representation of a woman blatantly displaying her sexual organs, would surely be unsuitable for any but the Black Mass. Moreover, many of these vessels are carved with extremely fragile projections, chiefly in the form of snakes, precisely in the position, just below the bowl, where they would need to be grasped if they were intended for use either as chalices (or ciboria) or as secular drinking cups.

When all factors are taken into account, it seems most probable that the examples first acquired by the British Museum (chiefly through the interest of Sir Augustus Wollaston Franks) in the middle of last century were correctly registered as 'salt cellars'. Their elaboration would be in character with that favoured by Renaissance craftsmen such as Cellini, for whom the salt cellar was frequently a vehicle for virtuosity.

As salt cellars these ivories would remain stationary in the middle of the table or perhaps be pushed across it by the base. Examples with two compartments presumably accommodated pepper also. Occasional Rabelaisian touches in the ornament would not be amiss.

THE HUNTING HORNS

These oliphants are, with only one or two exceptions, all end-blown, and not side-blown as are all other ivory trumpets made by the Negroes. We may take it as certain from this fact that they were made for the use of Europeans and not of Africans, however exalted. That they belong to the same style as the salt cellars is shown by the identity of the human figures which appear in the round or in high relief on some of them with those found on the bases of the vessels; and also by much of the strapwork and other non-figurative carving. Yet the principal decoration of the horns, namely the hunting scenes which are carved in low relief over the main surfaces, is appreciably different from anything to be found on the salt cellars, and is in fact of considerable interest on several counts. The heads of the human figures may seem to bear some family likeness (probably because they came from the same school of carvers) to the round figures of the cellars, but the features are never exaggerated to extreme prognathism as is normal in these latter. Then the figures of the hunters, their dogs and their prey, and the trees among which they hunt are disposed with exceptional freedom within the allotted panels, untethered in space by any ground line or trace of perspective (somewhat in the manner of the earliest Egyptian reliefs); even the bands of conventional raised ornament which define the panels are not absolute barriers, for in a fine oliphant at Stuttgart some of the animals are bisected by these bands.

I shall consider the origin of all these ivories in the final section of this text, but it will not be inappropriate to note here, while we are considering these hunting scenes, that they do not appear specifically African in any detail either of subject-matter or of treatment. The antlered deer and the wild boar which are the usual quarry of the chase are clearly of European species. The antelope is not found; when a lion is represented it wears a crown and is associated with harpies, wyverns and centaurs; and the elephant which appears on the Dresden oliphant not only has the small ears of the Indian species but bears an elaborate howdah on its back.

All these facts seem to suggest that they are translations into ivory of woodcut figures from early printed (or possibly manuscript) bestiaries and books on hunting and perhaps heraldry; I think it possible that they are close enough to the originals for these to be identified.

Of the spoons and the rarer forks little need be said. Their functional parts are of the forms which graced the aristocratic tables of sixteenth-century Europe; the ornamental parts conform—as can be seen—with our Afro-Portuguese style. Five excellent examples are in the Weickmann

Collection (formed in the early seventeenth century) at Ulm in South Germany, and the Musée de Cluny has a fork and a spoon, the latter of which is undoubtedly from the same hand or workshop as the British Museum spoon illustrated in our Plate 45, its handle terminating likewise in an inclined plate bearing an identical black-letter 'b'.

We are left only with those very few objects which are not subsumed in the preceding three groups. Of these the most important pieces known to me are the monstrous head shown in Plates 34 and 35, and another closely related to it, but slightly larger and more monstrous, in a New York private collection. To modern eyes these look like very suitable heads for apocryphal sea monsters, and indeed they oddly recall the famous oak prow of a Viking ship found in the Scheldt estuary and now in the British Museum. The function of these two pieces is enigmatic; they would make excellent handles for a knife or flywhisk, but in each the slightly convex basal surface is smooth and unpierced; they might conceivably have been used for crushing peppers at table. The Cluny powderhorn, already alluded to, is a crudely carved piece of work looking like a rather small oliphant and in fact rather similar in quality to one such in the National Museum of Lisbon.

THE IVORIES AND THEIR PLACE IN AFRICAN ART

THE VISUAL ART OF AFRICA CONSISTS—
if we leave out of account, as irrelevant to our purpose, the rock paintings and engravings left by more or less ancient Bushmen and others in North and South Africa and sporadically between—almost entirely of sculpture, for the most part in wood. However, this characteristic art of the Negroes is by no means evenly spread over Negro Africa: for reasons apparently historico-geographical, which need not detain us here, it is almost completely confined to the great basins of the Niger and the Congo—that is, to the area bounded on the north by the Sahara Desert, on the east by the Great Lakes and on the south by the Zambezi River and the Kalahari Desert. This area includes the great African rain forest, but also much open downland and even the semi-desert conditions of the Niger Bend. The economy of the area is predominantly agricultural, the coastal zones being in general the more fertile. Except for the nomadic Hamites of the Sudan and the Pygmies of the Congo, the inhabitants are Negroes of varying degrees of racial admixture with other peoples and are not readily classifiable into separate groups by purely physical criteria; they are more easily grouped by linguistic categories, most of the Niger peoples speaking Sudanic and the Congo peoples Bantu lan-

XV

guages — a dichotomy only slightly reflected in their general culture.

The sculpture of the Negroes does not follow a unitary tradition, as the art of post-tribal Europe has done; on the contrary, its most striking character is its diversity, and this indeed is almost the only common denominator of its innumerable styles. The European art tradition stems from Greek civilisation, and was merchanted to all Europe along the Roman roads; the network of communications of all kinds is a principal mark of the great continental civilisations and among other things it is the means by which aesthetic ideas and fashions travel from country to country and so bring about the assimilation of many national arts of various origin to form a single continental or international tradition in which local differences, though readily discernible, set off all the more notably its fundamental unity. The truth of this observation cannot be better illustrated than by noting the surprising extent to which, when Africans abandon their own traditions of tribal sculpture and turn to carving for the Europeans who come to them by way of modern communications, they suddenly conform to a single style which shows only slight local variation from the west coast to the east (and which is also to a great extent common to the tourist art of other continents, since in it the European characters are dominant and the indigenous characters recessive).

Anyone may see, from a comparison of the traditional and the tourist art of a tribe, that quite apart from the changes in outward form something more fundamental has been lost. This missing element appears, to me at least, to be the concept of dynamism, which provides the ontology, the philosophical basis, of the tribal way of life.

XVI

This view, which has probably been shared in some form by all peoples up to the onset of the more static conceptions inseparable from industrialism, interprets the world as consisting of energy rather than of matter, and makes man, and the rest of creation, subject to a struggle for existence in which a man's life-force is always waxing or waning, so that he must be constantly preoccupied with maintaining and increasing it. Tribal religions, therefore, are concerned not so much, as is commonly supposed, with human fertility in the narrow generative sense, but with the much broader idea of increase; phallic cults (which are in any case rare in Africa), ritual cannibalism and human sacrifice and other traits objectionable to Europeans, who regard them as more or less isolated superstitious practices, become more understandable when they are seen as part (though not a necessary part) of a coherent philosophy of vitalism. It is in this more general and elevated sense that the concept of increase, or dynamism, may be seen as a dominant mode in African sculpture, conditioning not only the subject-matter but the sculptural 'language', especially in the form of interpretations of the growth curves found in animal horns and tusks, claws, beaks and shells. Where fully tribal institutions prevail, the tribal cosmology is, normally, esoteric, in the sense that the tribesmen regard themselves in theory as the only true men, while other tribes with different regilions have to be ignored (for this purpose) because they are not subject to the sanctions of the tribal laws of nature; this applies still more to Europeans than to other tribes, since they survive and prosper without carrying out any increase ceremonies. Improved communications between tribes and with Europeans therefore tend to undermine tribal religions and the art which is to a great extent intimately linked with them. And when art comes to be practised for the benefit not of the tribalist but of the curio-hunting European, it is clear that the dynamistic content of the old art will not be applicable in the new situation and will be consciously or unconsciously dropped. Tourist art is in effect an imperfect projection of the European mind.

How far these observations are applicable to the case of the Afro-Portuguese ivories cannot well be determined until we know more of their place of origin and of the art forms, in West Africa and in Portugal, from which the hybrid was produced. Read and Dalton wrote in 1899: 'It is probable that if a large series of these fine African carvings could be brought together, there would be little difficulty in assigning them to their proper place of origin.' But the growth of the British Museum collection to some twenty pieces and the careful examination of at least as many more in other collections have not yet proved sufficient for the elucidation of the mystery.

I have adopted the term 'Afro-Portuguese' to express the common consent of scholars that these ivories were made to Portuguese orders by African craftsmen. On the one hand we find on many of the oliphants and salt cellars that the Portuguese arms are prominently displayed, as are less frequently the armillary sphere, which now forms part of the arms of Brazil, and the cross of the Knights of the Military Order of Christ; I have also found one salt cellar, at Oxford, which bears the *fleur-de-lys* as the principal decoration of the base.

On the other hand, the African craftsmanship is attested not only by the representation of Africans and African animals, but by African methods of stylising the figure and above all by an African technique of working the ivory: the carvings have the appearance of imitations of turned work, yet have in all cases been executed without use of the lathe (although in several cases it has been used later, presumably in Europe, in the course of repairs and alterations); and the European ivory-workers's traditional regard for the greatest possible naturalism of modelling and surface texture is eschewed in favour of the African sculptor's instinctive regard for moderation as expressed in a minimum measure for the scale of details.

While we may be sure that these works were carved by Africans, we cannot be sure that they were carved in Africa. The German scholar Wilhelm Foy advanced the view in 1901 that the oliphants were probably made, though no doubt by immigrant Negro craftsmen, in Portugal, and this might equally apply to the other objects. His article was a small counterblast to the opinion of Professor F. von Luschan, laid down with casual authority, unencumbered by evidence, shortly after the Benin Expedition of 1897, that these ivories were all Benin work; but this view has unaccountably continued to hold the field ever since, partly perhaps because the Benin canon of ivory-carving (as also of bronze-casting) was effectually obscured by the inclusion in it of Yoruba and other unrelated work, again under von Luschan's influence. In fact there is no similarity between Afro-Portuguese and Bini work, and I cannot discover that any piece or fragment in this style has been found at Benin, or indeed anywhere in Africa in modern times. It is easy to rule out Benin, but not to fix upon an alternative place of origin.

A process of comparison and elimination has led me to reduce to three the number of places on the west coast which have a claim to consideration. One of these is the area around what is now Freetown in Sierra Leone, where the Portuguese had a trading station at Mitombo; the treatment of the head in the Afro-Portuguese figures *(nomoli)* of Sierra Leone is remarkably similar, and though no real tradition of carving in ivory survives there, this is equally true of the *nomoli* themselves. Second is the Bakongo coast in the region of Loango and the Congo mouth, to which, until the Benin Expedition, these ivories were often attributed; the ivories known to come from there are not very close in style to those which we are considering, but could perhaps be regarded as a degeneration from the same style. Certainly the skill was there, and the sophistication, but no sufficiently clear piece of evidence has yet come to light to enable us to attach the style to the area with confidence. The third area is, in my view, the most promising: it is the old Slave Coast, and more specifically the towns of Lagos and Porto Novo, or perhaps Whydah, the port of the Kingdom of Dahomey. In this case the makers would have been Yoruba, and there are certain stylistic points which favour this tentative identification: the form of the human heads, with drawn-out prognathous faces, strongly suggests the Gelede Society masks of the western Yoruba; some of the ivory relief figures (e.g. Plates 19—21) are like miniature representations of the well-known *ibeji* figures carved in memory of dead twin children; some figures wear cloth caps of Yoruba type (which, however, are like those worn by the Mandingo peoples of Sierra Leone and elsewhere); and in many cases the lips are shown parallel, not converging to a point at the corners (see especially Plates 21, 23, 27—29), normally a reliable diagnostic feature of Yoruba style (but again, unfortunately, found, though more rarely, both in some *nomoli* and in Baleongo work).

Though no certainty has yet been achieved, it is possible at any time that a piece will come to light which exhibits some decisive feature; in a New York private collection is a salt cellar on which a man sits on a seat of peculiar construction, and this may yet prove to be identifiable. There must be many examples still in private hands, some unidentified even as African, and perhaps the publication of this book in which the style is isolated for the first time will lead to further knowledge.

Négrerie is a term unknown to art historians, familiar though they are with *chinoiserie* and *japonaiserie*. In these ivories made for the Portuguese nobles is found its first and most successful manifestation (if we leave out of account some passing fashions in Greek and Roman times): like the works of Carl Fabergé, they may be regarded as a perversion of art, but one supremely well executed. We may be grateful to the sixteenth-century Portuguese for their good taste, for in later times hybridism in African art has taken far less harmonious forms, in the curios mass-produced for the naïve traveller. And on a more sophisticated level, where the interior decorator is the *arbiter elegantiarum,* the cult of *négrerie* flourishes exceedingly, while true appreciation of the art of Africa is the privilege of a discerning few.

THE MOST COMPREHENSIVE PUBLICATION of Afro-Portuguese ivories before the present volume was contained in *Antiquities from the City of Benin and from the other Parts of West Africa, in the British Museum,* by Sir Hercules Read and O. M. Dalton, published by the Museum in 1899. The pieces concerned (all—except those on pages 32 and 34—also published in this volume) are illustrated on Plates I, II, 2 and 5, III, IV, 2 and V (the remaining pieces on Plates II and IV are of traditional eastern Yoruba origin), and on pages 32, 34, 36 and 38. They are discussed on pages 14 and 33–9, but the authors unfortunately did not distinguish very clearly between the Afro-Portuguese on the one hand and traditional Yoruba and Bini work on the other, being more than half inclined to attribute the former to Benin itself.

Felix von Luschan in his *Altertümer von Benin,* 3 vols., 1919, discusses these hybrid ivories briefly on pages 478 and 479 of Vol. I, and illustrates important examples in the collections of the Museum für Völkerkunde, Berlin, on Plates 119 and 120 (and perhaps Plate 116*a,* a side-blown hunting horn) of Vol. III.

Two important salt cellars in American collections are illustrated, as

Nos. 127 and 128, in the exhibition catalogue *Masterpieces of African Art*, Brooklyn, 1954. Spoons in the Ulm collection are illustrated in an article in Baessler-Archiv, Vol. IV. Part 1, pages 29—38, by R. Andree, who also describes the Brunswick collection of four spoons and a salt cellar in *Globus*, Vol. LXXIX, No. 10, 1901, pages 156—9. J. E. Lips publishes one of the Brunswick spoons and a middle portion of a salt cellar at the Royal Scottish Museum, Edinburgh, in *The Savage Hits Back*, London, 1937, figs. 123, 148. F. Heger published in *Mitt. d. Wiener Anthrop. Ges.*, Vol. 29, 1899, pages 61—9, illustrations of a salt cellar, part of another, six spoons and a fork in the Vienna collection. Of three salt cellars (only one complete) and four spoons at Copenhagen, the finest salt cellar is published in *Guides to the National Museum: Primitive Tribes of the Tropics*, Copenhagen, 1941, page 101. The foregoing references are only a selection from a larger number.

Wilhelm Foys's doubts about the Benin origin of the ivories are published in *Abhandl. v. Ber. des Kgl. Zool. v. A. E. Museums, Dresden*, Vol. 9, 1900—01, pages 20—22.

THE PLATES

An ivory vessel, believed to be a salt cellar for European use, purchased by the British Museum in 1867.

This piece, certainly among the finest known examples of the style, was carved from an exceptionally massive tusk; height $9\frac{1}{4}$ inches.

Detail of the lid, illustrating a vein of grisly humour not uncommon in, for example, Yoruba art.

Detail of the base; the four male and four female figures may all represent Africans.

The women's body scarifications are somewhat like those of Bakongo women near the mouth of the Congo.

The four men wear European dress but are given African features. Their pious attitude suggests a satire on hypocrisy.

This fine vessel, $11\frac{3}{4}$ inches high, has two nearly globular compartments, perhaps for salt and pepper.

The ship represented on the lid is curiously simplified, as though imitated from a fifteenth-century woodcut.

A man is seen in the ship's crow's nest; the thickened sheets or ropes are an African feature.

On each side appears a presumably Portuguese knight or other dignitary with a deferential attendant.

An attendant (left) and a knight carrying a spear (right). The carving was presented in 1878.

The surviving middle section, presented in 1879, of a treatment of the same subject by another hand.

Detail of Plate 12: head of a Portuguese knight. A third middle section, perhaps by the same hand as the complete example, is in the Museum für Völkerkunde, Berlin.

Another double salt cellar, generally of the same form as that shown in Plates 7—11 but differing in subject.

14

Two armed Portuguese horsemen are attended by a smaller Portuguese and by a naked African figure.

The carving is $8\frac{3}{4}$ inches high, but the cover is later European turned work. It was purchased in 1856.

The same carving from the back. The relief designs on the undersides of the two compartments include European faces; the upper sphere represents a tree.

17

One of the two Portuguese knights. Detail of salt cellar shown in Plates 14–17. This subject is treated by an inferior hand in a piece at Berlin, lacking the base portion but with original lid.

A fine example, $7\frac{1}{2}$ inches high, of the type of salt cellar with conical base and main ornament plainly of European derivation.

The figures of trousered women suggest Yoruba wood-carving style (though Yoruba women do not nowadays wear trousers).

The snakes confronting snarling dogs (usually more recognisable) are a constant feature of this form of salt cellar.

This unusual salt cellar, 11 inches high, was presented in 1869 by Sir Augustus Wollaston Franks, Keeper of Antiquities.

On the hat and around the projections on the conical lid are coiled three eel-like creatures.

The Janus head, rare in Europe, is a recurring motif in African sculpture, from the Senegal to the Zambezi.

The five nude figures presumably represent Africans, some wearing European hats (the leftmost figure has been supplied by a restorer).

This base is related to that shown in Plate 33, and both have much affinity with Yoruba work.

This salt cellar, acquired in 1952 and $6\frac{1}{8}$ inches high, has lost its base, the present foot having been turned.

The Janus theme appears again, though in African art the heads are more commonly of opposite sex.

The Yoruba-like treatment of the lips and other features is especially evident in this piece.

When acquired in 1871 this remarkable cover was attached by European brass mountings to part of a Yoruba ivory armlet.

The monstrous quadruped may be a caricatured and partly anthropomorphised dog; the Janus head above suggests rather animalised humanity.

As often in this art, the surface enhancement of the animal is like that on the lid proper; height $4\frac{1}{2}$ inches.

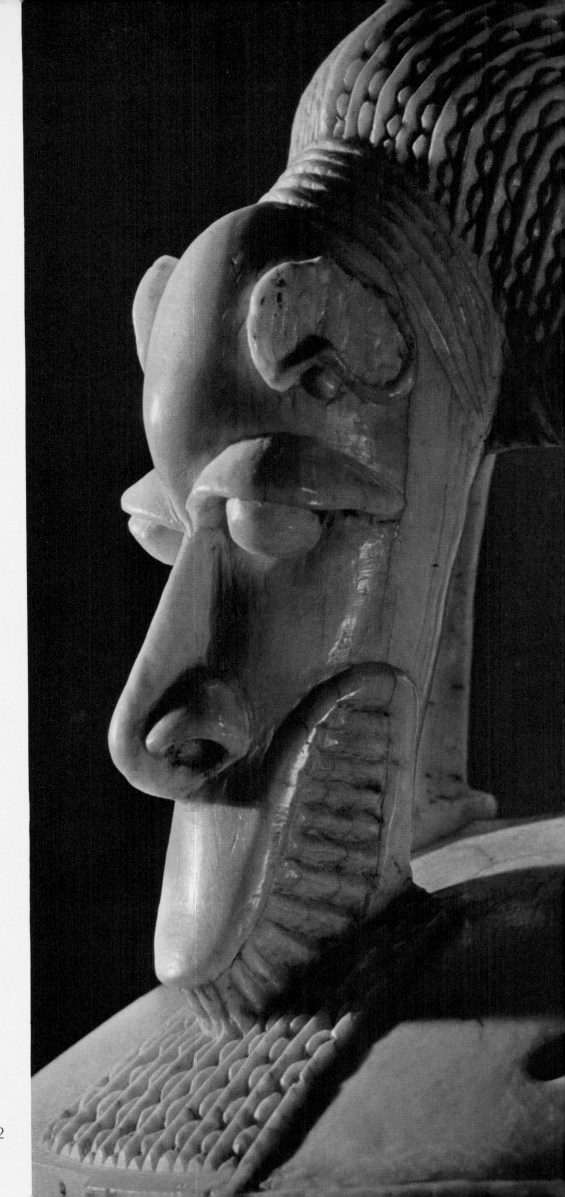

This small ($4\frac{5}{8}$ inches) salt cellar is perhaps the most Yoruba-like of all and certainly the most heavily worn.

This monstrous head, $4\frac{1}{2}$ inches high, was presented in 1874 by Franks, who formed the greater part of this collection.

The use of this carving is obscure, though the unpierced, slightly convex base could be used for crushing pepper.

This end-blown oliphant, $22\frac{1}{2}$ inches long, of translucent thinness and unusually open design, bears the arms of Portugal on each side.

Here the Portuguese arms are accompanied on the other side by the armillary sphere; the horn is 19 inches long.

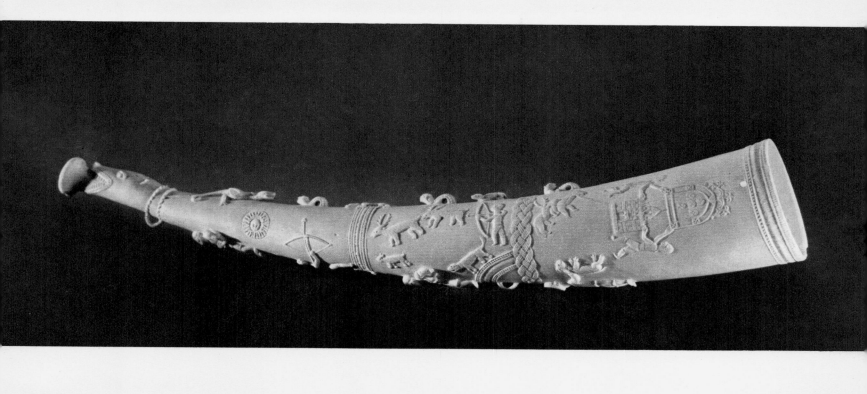

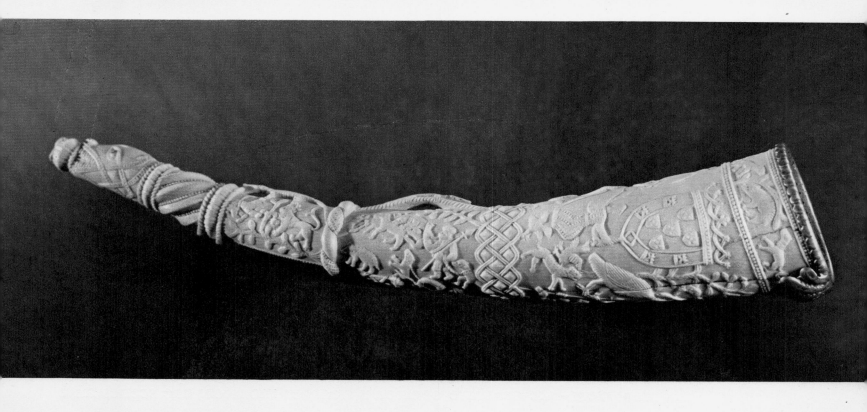

A wyvern-like creature confronts another monster; the scenes and animals represented have no recognisably African character.

These hunting scenes may have been inspired by European book illustrations rather than by direct observation.

The bowl of this spoon reproduces European metal forms; a helix shell in a snake's mouth terminates the handle; length $9\frac{1}{4}$ inches.

Forks are much rarer than spoons; a dog-like animal bites a snake which confronts a crocodile; length $9\frac{1}{2}$ inches.

The handle here ends in a dog's head, but part of the ornament is broken away; length $10\frac{1}{4}$ inches.

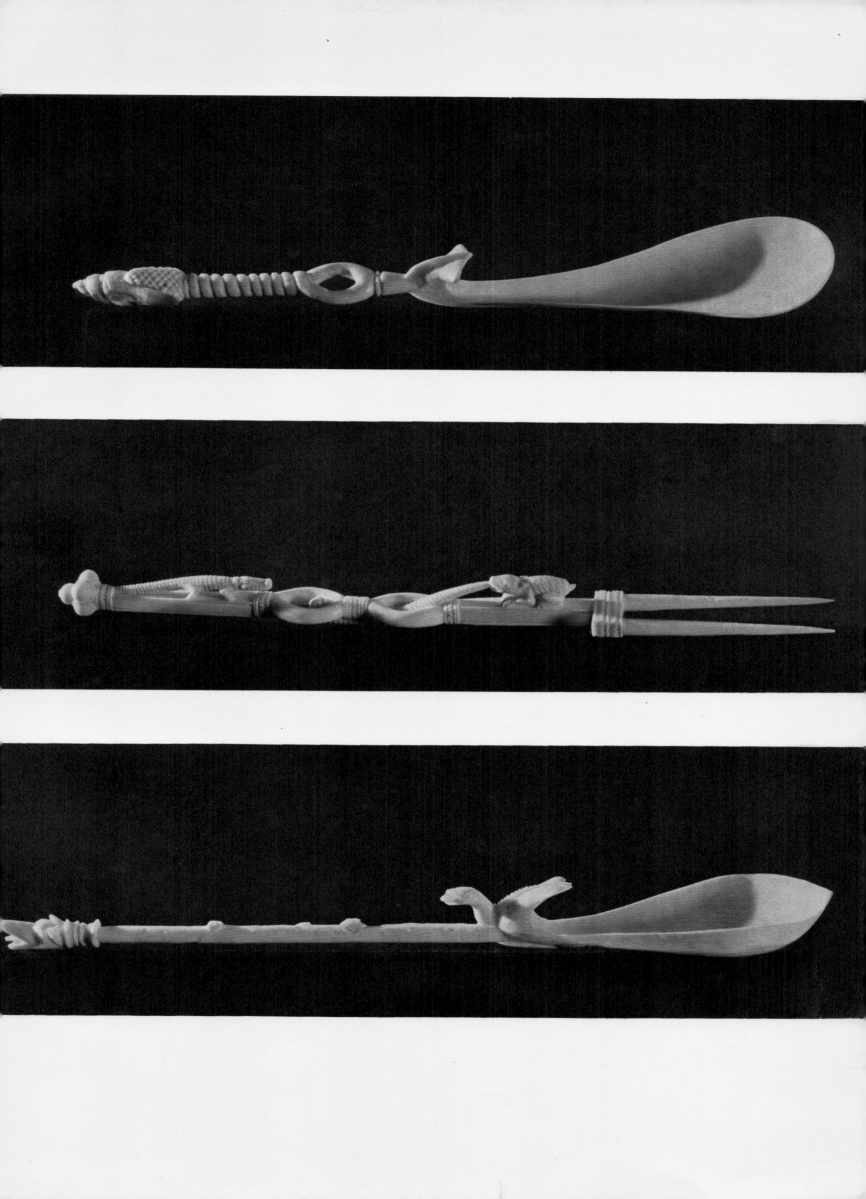

The bowl is here so thin that a paper label is seen through it; length $10\frac{1}{8}$ inches.

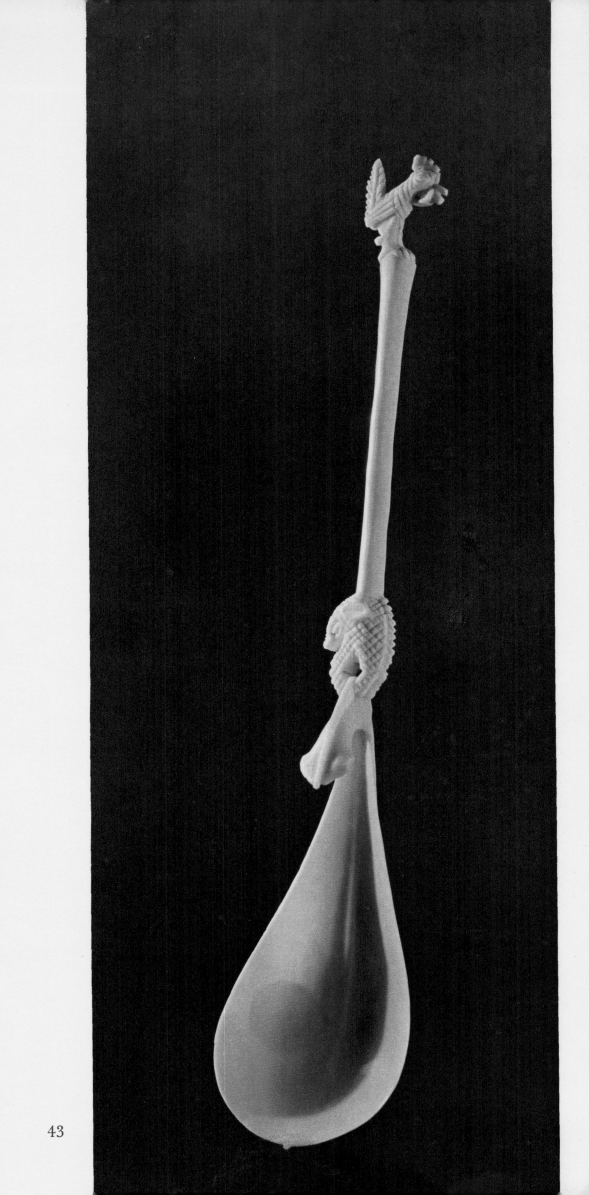

43

The figure-of-eight is a typically African form of virtuosity; a crocodile lies along the handle; length $9\frac{1}{2}$ inches.

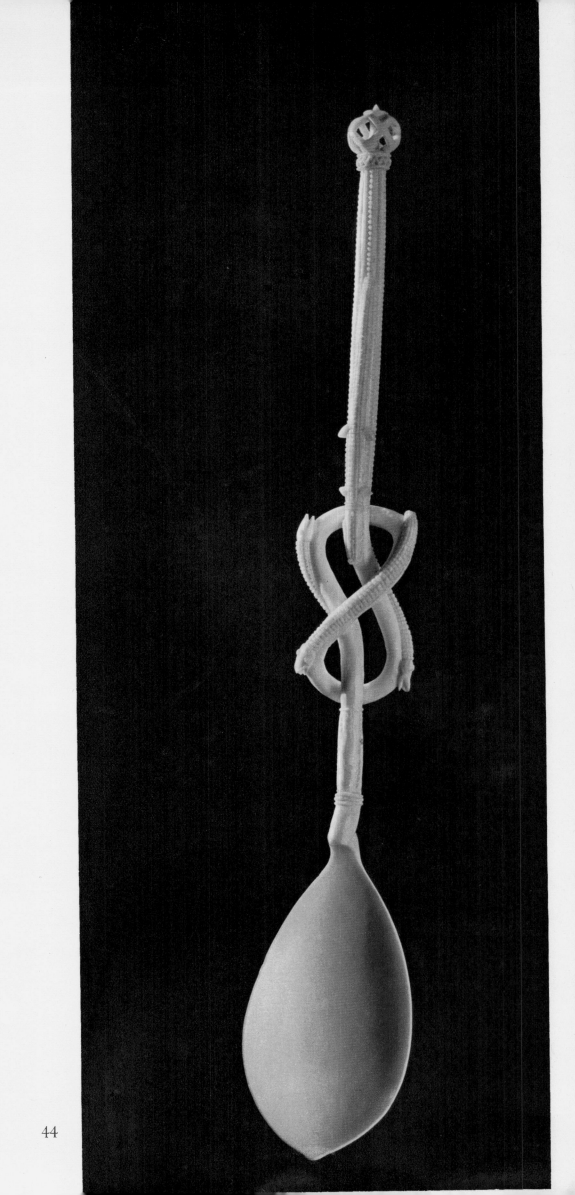

The handle of a spoon at Cluny with similar bowl and identical terminating cipher as the one depicted here has two figures-of-eight; length $8\frac{3}{8}$ inches.

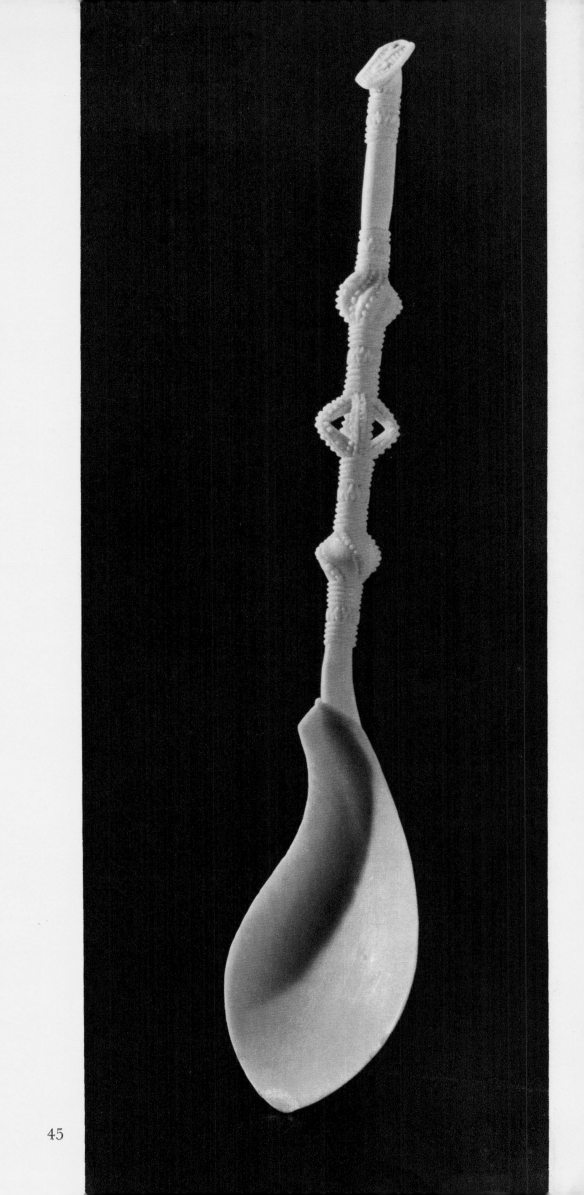

The lively barefooted figure, perhaps a Portuguese page, is carved in African proportion with enlarged head; length $7\frac{3}{4}$ inches.